The Progressiv of James

Charles E. Morris

Alpha Editions

This edition published in 2024

ISBN 9789362511843

Design and Setting By
Alpha Editions
www.alphaedis.com
Email - info@alphaedis.com

As per information held with us this book is in Public Domain.
This book is a reproduction of an important historical work.
Alpha Editions uses the best technology to reproduce historical work
in the same manner it was first published to preserve its original nature.
Any marks or number seen are left intentionally to preserve.

Contents

CHAPTER I	- 1 -
CHAPTER II	- 4 -
CHAPTER III	- 8 -
CHAPTER IV	- 14 -
CHAPTER V	- 30 -
CHAPTER VI	- 34 -
CHAPTER VII	- 41 -
CHAPTER VIII	- 45 -
CHAPTER IX	- 48 -

CHAPTER I

THE NEED FOR A DOER

There come times in the affairs of men which call for "not a forgetful hearer, but a doer of the work." Such a time is at hand. A great war, the most devastating in history, has been concluded. Its moral lesson has been taught by its master minds and learned in penitence, we may hope, by the erring and wrongly willful. But the fruits of victory are ungathered and the beneficence of peace is not yet attained. The call arises for a "doer of the work."

Two great political parties in the United States, both with splendid accomplishments behind them and both with grave mistakes as well, have attempted to respond to this call, and America, whose proudest boast is that it has always found a man for every great occasion, chooses between them. It is a solemn and serious hour. For it has been America's special fortune that its great teachers and leaders and doers have been found at just the proper time.

This knowledge of the certain right decision of our country is, we might almost say, a part of its very fiber abiding with the persistency of a fixed idea, a part of the heritage of the nation, scarcely needing to be taught in the schools, obvious even to the casual student from an alien land. For our historical records glow with the stories of the appearance of *the* man; and the thought of a friendly destiny seems not easy to banish. Time has given so often either the inspired teacher of the word or the doer of the work that there is more than a faith and a hope, nay almost a conviction, that it cannot fail now when the agonized appeal of the world beckons America to complete her high mission to humanity upon which she embarked when she threw her power and might on the scales in war.

Those who insist that the fulfillment of that mission lies in keeping the solemn promises make in France, accepted by friend and foe alike, for a League of Nations to end war, to see that retribution becomes not blind vengeance, to set the tribes of the earth again on their forward journey, present as their leader James Monroe Cox, Governor of Ohio.

A party of traditions, a party that has directed in every critical period save one since the Republic began, has said that he meets the requirements of the time. That party chose him because of his record for doing, because there was an inner conviction that he could enter upon a still larger field with a growing, an ever-expanding capacity.

This, too, furnishes a fitter chapter in the history of country and party. For the wise selection of men, even obscure men, has been the tower of our national strength. America had her Thomas Jefferson to expound for all the world the real underlying truth of her Revolution. The equality of rights and duties spread from a dream of philosophers to be the doctrine of warriors for freedom. There was her George Washington to hold together the tenuous bands of freedom. She found her James Monroe to lay the foundations of the doctrine that stern moral precepts forbid the violation of sovereign rights of the nations. She brought forth her Andrew Jackson to make the country in his time safe for democracy, and to establish for all time that no single money baron, nor yet any collection of them, is superior to the power of all the people.

In later time she had her Abraham Lincoln, now in the judgment of the succeeding generations but little beneath the Savior of men, preserver of the Union for its larger duties. She had in this day her Woodrow Wilson, builder of the newer policy of world union and recognized spokesman of freedom in the death struggle with military autocracy. It is of history that Lincoln and Wilson both were stricken down with their work incomplete. After Lincoln there was no doer of the work to finish his task and the evil of those who perverted the exalted purpose of the Civil War continues even unto this day.

Coming into the arena of national affairs when even America seems to doubt and when the selfish motive of fear threatens to palsy the nation's hand, Governor Cox became the man to vindicate the statements and the pledges given before all the world. His introduction to the conscience and intellect of the country was a demand that the faith be kept.

Out of the night of war, the League of Nations has long been a supreme issue with Governor Cox and he was chosen to carry the standard because he had expressed the sentiment most strongly, most clearly and with greatest emphasis.

Doers have ever been practical men, and such is Governor Cox. But practicality need not, and does not, imply a lack of vision. There is such a thing as ideality in vision and a practical hand to make good the picture of the mind. The combined qualities are considered as essentials to the adequate man of the times, for a vision of a new world order is the rarest gift of the century, but the man with the dynamic force and the cunning skill to make this new dream come true has been wanting.

History—political history—was changed profoundly when President Woodrow Wilson was stricken. Men were slow in rallying to his cause, there were even clouds of doubt, ominous and disturbing, when the party he led to two victories prepared in the late June and the early July days of the year 1920 to state its position, its hope and its aspirations.

In the state in which Governor Cox held leadership there was no doubt. His own Ohio knew long ago that at the Democratic National Convention in San Francisco its chosen spokesmen would communicate but two mandates on behalf of the vast majority of the people. One was that Ohio could do no less than be faithful to its greatest executive and the other was that the nation's faith and honor must be kept stainless.

Through Governor Cox that message has been sent to the length and breadth of the land. As seen by him, the appeal to the American people is one which began with the first plea to the world powers for such a concert as would banish the continual threat of war. This plea was made to warring powers when the World War began in 1914 and it was renewed at each favorable opportunity during the years when America hoped that the war might be brought to an end before the last great neutral power was drawn into it. Heeded by the Allies, the voice of reason was rejected by the Central Empires, and from that hour there came the conviction among the earnest lovers of peace that only the imposition of peace would furnish a new basis for world concord.

Few men were more downcast than this same man when long and vexatious delays in the United States Senate ended at last in the recalcitrant refusal of the masters of the majority to ratify the Treaty of Versailles. It is but a fair and truthful statement to observe that, although his judgment of the mind of the people told him that the party which went before the country to vindicate the sacrifices of the men in the trenches would have a most compelling issue, he had no wish for such partisan advantage. As a Democrat, history will tell that he sought only fair compromise on the treaty, even suggesting any honest settlement that would hasten America's entrance into the League.

In his address of acceptance, then, Governor Cox stepped to the fore with the tersest of utterances as to his position on the League, compressing it all into "I favor going in."

If this question is not answered now and affirmatively, Governor Cox believes that there may be delay until nations once more have borne their crosses on Calvary and until further blood and treasure are wasted. And so he says now: "I favor going in."

CHAPTER II

COX THE MAN

Men of great versatility are most difficult to picture comprehensively. Perhaps this is the reason that no pen-portrait of Theodore Roosevelt ever seemed quite complete. There was in every single sketch something that seemed to be left unsaid, a point made by one was certain to be omitted by another. Cox is a man after the Roosevelt type. They were fast friends and they had many ideas in common. They often exchanged views upon progressive issues and found themselves largely in accord. Neither was static in mental processes and their dynamics were often of the same sort.

But while Governor Cox's intimates compare him often with Roosevelt, they prefer to liken him to Andrew Jackson. For Cox is the true Twentieth Century Jacksonian, they say. Like Andrew Jackson, Governor Cox can improvise the organization of a political campaign better than any man of his time, save Colonel Roosevelt, and the masterful Colonel won only when he had great resources at his command. Cox seems to have reached back into history and grasped the idea of the manner in which Jackson's men worked with resources so small that they had to pass newspapers of their faith from hand to hand.

Largely, it seems, because no war came along when he was free of family responsibilities Governor Cox has no martial record. He might have been a soldier of the Roosevelt type had he lived in other circumstances but his youth was spent in the drudgery of toil and there was no chance for education in a military academy.

Still they call him "fighting Jimmy," and those who have been through a campaign with him know what they mean. As a boy there was never need to drive him forward to personal combat and in the man the juvenile tendency continued until he was well past the forty-five-year mark of middle age.

If one were to inventory his external features there would appear a compact, muscular individual of about five feet six inches in height and of one hundred and seventy pounds in weight, every ounce keyed up to the efficiency of successful performance. motions indicate a man of quick decision, a tendency to suddenness that many older than he have sought to check in his earlier years. It is a proverb among those who know him best that when Governor Cox makes an instant decision he may be mistaken but that when he thinks it over for a single night he is never wrong. As the years in a varied experience have passed this disposition to think everything over has grown and grown until snap judgments no longer are taken. This may be the reason why men say that he has improved as an executive from year to year and why his later acts and deeds have the rounded out and complete aspect that is lacking in the earlier. The nature of Cox himself is for "action," even when it seems to take the form of experiment. In simple justice it must be said that he has never been an adventurer, but he is willing to tackle problems before other would seize hold of them. His first administration, he thinks, was his best, for much more was done, but his last is his best, Ohio judgment has decided, because it repressed tendencies to go the wrong way, taking perhaps the Gladstone view that a statesman deserves more credit for defeating unwise legislation than for securing the enactment of good. As Governor, Cox has been willing to risk defeat for principle.

A trait of character is told in the story of school and taxation legislation. He was warned that progressive steps would encompass his defeat. If a composite answer could be formed to all the suggestions of this sort, it would be something like this: "There is need for improving our schools. Time will vindicate it."

Something else of character may be learned from the manner in which Governor Cox redeems pledges. When he was sorely beset by his political foes in 1914, it was represented to him that the liquor interests might be made to do service if licenses were withheld until after the election. And the answer given was something like this: "The pledge was given that the license system shall not be prostituted to partisanship. That pledge will be redeemed."

The forebodings of the worldly wise were not disappointed. The liquor interests contributed heavily to the opposition candidate and supported him so well that he won the election.

Cox hates war even if he made a remarkable record as war Governor. But he likes the smoke and fury of political contest, and he thrives on campaigns. He has a fashion of leading his party organization and making it do his will, and like all men or this sort, he has been accused of being dictatorial. Yet none denies that he gives a fair hearing and is open to conviction on disputed issues.

He has a power of expression in a few words, portraying a whole field of action. Tending to go into great detail in public matters, he comes to the heart of an issue with a laconic expression that tells all there is to be told. "I favor going in"—on the League of Nations is one. Assuring his supporters that the proposal for separate peace with Germany was "opening their front lines," he drew a word sketch of a gigantic contest in which he as a general had sensed a rift in the opposition ranks and had broken through a whole army.

Associates of Governor Cox say that he is daring because of his strong sense of justice. The question is frequently asked by him as to whether a proposition is fair to all sides. Readiness to trust in him as an arbitrator has brought many issues to his desk that are not part of a Governor's official duties. Disputes between interests and differences among organizations, no less than capital and labor disagreements have been left to his decision. It is an evidence of the trust in the sense of justice in the man.

There is a notable habit in him of picking men quickly for tasks. It is not claimed for him that he has never made mistakes in his estimate of men, but they are comparatively rare.

Governor Cox is the only man ever nominated for President who owns wealth—real wealth. His personal fortune is handsome. That was a point of criticism when he began to get acquainted with the country, but it is no longer. The reason is to be found in the fact that he has a natural appeal that makes his associates forget money. Nor is the charge ever seriously made that his broad sympathy is affected. When he is best known, the wealth he owns is least often mentioned.

They do not refer to a wealthy man whose possessions are an outstanding attribute as "Jim" or "Jimmy." Cox, the man of affairs, is overshadowed by "Jimmy Cox."

As with all powerful leaders, no sketch would be complete if it did not allude to a certain imperiousness that is in the man. This quality has made foes but that was inevitable. One who has risen by his own efforts has had the pushing impulse, of course.

It tells something of the Cox character that he has become a forceful speaker only in the last ten years. When he first entered public life in 1908 his style in speaking lacked force and his manner was hesitating and uncertain. A course of self- discipline and training led to constant improvement, and while there has never been a pretense of oratorical flight, issues and questions are discussed plainly and effectively. There is a penchant for reducing statements to simple and understandable terms and for stating his conviction with a measure of aggressiveness that carries conviction.

As a candidate he has always believed that the people are entitled to the fullest information possible and to see and hear those who seek their suffrage.

Like Roosevelt, the more strenuous sports and recreations attract him far more that does the swinging of the golf stick. He is an expert marksman and has astonished military men on the rifle range by what he can do with a gun. His ancestors were squirrel-hunters, and his sure eye was an inheritance from them. The Governor likes to rough it in the Northern Canadian woods, spending at leisure a couple of weeks with only his son, James M. Jr., now a boy of 18, for his companion. He prides himself upon his ability to cook a fish after it is caught, and to plunge in the lake as an evidence of his swimming ability. When in Columbus his form of exercise is walking, and younger men of sedentary pursuits find that he can tire them.

Quitting school at an early age, Cox's education has been acquired through much private study. He knows no language except English. His range of reading covers a wide variety of topics, the favorite of which are the political sciences, and outdoor life. He does not lay claim to literary excellence or perfection of style, and is a man of serious bent of mind, speaking only when he thinks he has a message to carry.

The name under which he has been known to the country, James Middleton Cox, seems to be an error which only lately his friends have corrected. In the old family Bible the name of James Monroe Cox appears, indicative of a family admiration. The name which appears signed to all official documents is James M. Cox. The Middleton seems to have had its origin in a bit of journalistic levity, probably having reference to Middletown, Ohio, the city in which he got his early training as a newspaper reporter.

The Governor's family consists of his wife, a little daughter, Anne, who is slightly less than a year old, a married daughter, Mrs. Daniel J. Mahoney of Dayton, and two sons, James M. Jr., and John, age ten.

While the Governor's devotion to the equal suffrage cause has been of many years' standing, the interests of Mrs. Cox are of a domestic nature. The time not devoted to her baby daughter is spent in the outdoors, he hobby being her garden.

CHAPTER III

WHY COX IS A CANDIDATE FOR PRESIDENT

James M. Cox is a candidate for President because he hopes to be the instrument of divine Providence in a great accomplishment. He knows that the man who secures America's adherence to the League of Nations is as certain of a permanent place in the scrolls of fame as those who laid the foundations of freedom or those who preserved it in the days of fiery trial. To a famous correspondent, Mr. Herbert Corey, who put the question, "Why do you wish to be President?" The Governor has answered: "It affords an opportunity to take hold of a knotty situation (the League) by the back of the neck and seat of the pants and shake a result out of it."

The answer rings true to the man. The candidate has called it an issue of supreme faith, elaborating his views in a recent communication to the "Christian Herald," in which he has said:

"'Fighting the good fight of faith'—these words from the epistle to Timothy might well be our text for this campaign before the American people, which, within the limits of our strength, has been carried to every fireside in this broad land of ours. Ours is a fight of faith—faith with a world that accepted our statement of unselfish purpose, faith with fathers and mothers, wives and loved ones, who gave their sons, husbands and brothers to war upon war, faith with those who made sacrifice in homes, faith with those who toiled, faith with the living and faith with the dead.

"If there were in this contest nothing but the question of whether one or the other of two editors should sit in the seat of power, nothing but whether one organization or another should taste the sweets of office, we could not insist that there is involved a fight of faith. There is, indeed, an issue between two views of government, one looking forward and the other backward. But temporary control by one side or the other for a brief period of four years is not necessarily a supreme matter of faith. We might try one or we might, in a spirit of experiment, try another.

"In speaking of this we would have our personal fortunes forgotten. They are of transient interest to ourselves and we might say of less interest to others. To hold the exalted office of President of the United States, to occupy the place of Washington, of Jefferson, of Lincoln, to be looked to for leadership in public questions, to be the first citizen in this great land is not a trifling but a gigantic ambition, worthy of all honest striving but involving, in the ordinary sense, no supreme issue. So if personal reasons only animated us, we could not muster the temerity to state our case with the ardent zeal that controls us.

"But the motives that guide us are of greater import. As leader of a great organization which has had its part in interpreting the aspirations of the American people, and in shaping Americanism through the generations we have been invested with a sacred commission, a mandate sanctified by the reckless bravery of our sons and ennobled by the heart impulses of our daughters. Through circumstances not of our own choosing we have become the custodians of the honor of the nation, we have been called to fight the good fight of faith.

"We as a party willed otherwise. In the face of bigoted denials of our good faith we sought only concord of all our people in the tasks of American in the world. There was glory enough for all and we never advanced the claim that it was a partisan matter until the fact had been established through long and weary months of purposeful misunderstanding and unconscionable intrigue for party advantage by our opponents. There is in this no suggestion of unkind sentiments toward our leading adversaries. We can utter the sentiment voiced on the hill above Jerusalem and when America has come to understand we stand ready to blot out a dark chapter of our national life and to pronounce a pardon upon a course of conduct charitably covered by 'they know not what they do.'

"There ought to be in this a special appeal to believers in the living faith. Its purpose to give to all the universal benefits only a share of which it claims for itself, its conception of the Golden Rule as the practical basis for dealings with the world, its high plan to save the weak and feeble from the power and will of the mighty—these things, we say, are of the very essence of the true faith.

"It is not a subject for marvel then that practically every denominational and interdenominational gathering of religious men that has been held since the Versailles covenant was adopted has included an endorsement of that great document. Aloof from the contentions of partisans, freed from the bigotry engendered by factionalism, looking upon national questions through the windows of light and truth, the banded followers of the Man of Nazareth have seen the question that is presented shorn of false claims. In a word, Christians, speaking organically, with a voice that could not be misunderstood have stated that they wish the League of Nations.

"For such a League, for the only league now in existence or which has a fair chance of coming into existence, we are contending. Could the question be lifted from the arena of partisanship and could the referendum which we have invoked be by direct ballot, there would be no opposition. Unfortunately, our system of government has not provided a choice so direct, nor a manner of expression that would leave so small doubt as to the sentiment of America. We say this from a field of personal experience for like the certain rich young man of Biblical story, we, too, have seen the type of uncompromising partisan who 'turned away sorrowfully' for party seemed more important than duty or honor.

"It matters little whether we say that we feel deeply for those across the seas in their troubles when we fail to act in their behalf. The successful issue of the war left a duty on our hands, a duty like that which we performed in Cuba nearly a generation ago and like that which has been brought close to completion in the Philippines. We faced a Christian duty toward our associates and even toward the people of enemy lands. It was our obligation to bind up the wounds of the war and to show by example the fulfillment of high ideals voiced by the leaders of the world thought.

"There came to us the divine opportunity to act quickly and with high Christian purposes. We might with one stroke have become the counselor and friend of all humanity, its guarantor that all the forces of morality would be enlisted upon the side of peace. But the precious moments were wasted in fruitless discussion, in idle bickerings, in invention of fancied situations, purposely forgetting that the great purpose of the League of Nations was to band the world together in a great brotherhood against war. We were to lead the nations back to peaceful ways but through our own wavering we actually, by reason or a small coterie of men, we think wrongly advised, have drenched Europe and Asia with new wars.

"The great heart of America has always been right upon this great issue. There has never been a time when associations of men and women, independent of partisanship, have turned from the League proposal. America gave freely in alms to every war-torn nation in the world. She sent her devoted bands of workers to relieve distress. She sent her nurses to heal the sick. She sent her contributions to feed the hungry. She opened her warehouses to clothe the naked. She willingly gave her talent, through private auspices, to help bring life back to normal. Her men of finance gave counsel; they offered credit and we applauded. We were touched by the works of associations and individuals to lessen war's terrors and to refound the wrecked civilization. But foolish men, vain men, envious men forbade our government to do in larger form the same sort of acts which, done by private auspices, we applauded as evidence of Christian purpose.

"And the good that we sought to do was lost in our larger neglect. Weak fears that in helping the world, fantastic forebodings that in taking our stand for peace everlasting, imaginary perils that in service we might be surrendering our birthright of independence restrained our more noble impulses. While famine stalked and the world cried to heaven for our help we debated selfish questions. Our nation became a silent but effective partner in undermining Christian civilization, causing the despairing peoples of Europe, friend and enemy alike, to turn in every agony to those who denied the fundamental precepts upon which our society rests.

"Some one has called this black despair, 'Satanism,' the belief that the laws and deeds of God and men are set against the victim. And we, through the perversity of a few men, have been silent enemies of Christian faith and allies, indeed, or this newer scourge of mankind. There are happiness and satisfaction in the thought that we have not this fault to bear. It is not strange to us that those who permitted narrow views and ungenerous purpose to thwart our nation in its duty rest uncomfortably under the accusations of the American conscience. If temporary success is to be won at such sacrifice we cannot think it worth the price.

"Nor can the blame be shifted. So far as was humanly possible, objections were met. Reservations stating our complete compliance with the fundamental organic law, needless as they were in a strictly legal sense, were proposed. Others were accepted where they seemed to be animated by proper motives, but good faith prevented acceptance of those which proposed to withdraw the pledge in the same document in which it was plighted. As was observed in the address accepting the designation as champion of the party, every boy in our schools knows that war may be declared only by act of Congress and that the American Constitution rises superior to all treaties. Still, every friend of the Covenant was ready to acquiesce in proposals that would state these propositions, and more, if that would prove a solution.

"Failing in this effort, the resolution was formed that the only other method lay in submitting the matter in a solemn referendum to the conscience of America. In that great judgment we now are. Men are but instrumentalities of the Divine Will, worked out, we pray, in the nations. Few things are of smaller importance than the temporal fortunes of men; no things of greater importance than the destiny of mankind. Willingly would we undergo crushing defeat to save the principle for which we strive, guiltily would we assume power won by appeal to baser motives and selfish fears.

"There is in this year, for the causes here outlined, a militancy as of the Crusaders, marching over mountains and deserts to wrest the Holy Places from unworthy hands. There is a sacred fire in the countenances of those who speak the message, there is a joy in proclaiming the tidings, there is a zeal in spreading the word. We are preachers this year of national righteousness, of honor, of faith and of high purpose.

"We scorn to think of our mission in ordinary terms. We disdain to look upon the early days of November as a test of rival organizations in their power to muster votes. We have no mind to compete in lavish outlay, we have no purpose to resort to sinister methods of electrical appeal. If we are to be chosen, it is to be because we have won the conscience of the nation, and God helping us, we will appeal to nothing else.

"We turn from the external duties of the country to its internal. Promises with respect to these matters must of every necessity be in general terms largely because the problems are vast and must adjust themselves to all parts of the country, harmonizing with conditions that vary widely. Back of all legislation, back of statute and executive policy worth while, there lies one unvarying hope and purpose—to right wrong, to secure justice and to give equal opportunity. All measures must be tested by these great principles and on them rest securely if at all.

"Past performances—the record—furnish the best indication of a man's mind, and the executive acts and legislative recommendations of the Governor of Ohio during the past six years have been studied with great care. That they have won approval is a source of gratification and satisfaction that will endure. We are in this country face to face with gigantic problems. They cannot be left unsolved. That would be blindness. They cannot be considered in the gathering darkness of reaction, they must be viewed in the brightening dawn of a new day.

"Before us we have the examples of restrained liberties and of unfulfilled desires. It is dangerous to trust reactionary forces with power. It may become a little short of menacing to the stability of our institutions and to the orderly processes of development. It is well to sound a word of warning, calmly but ever seriously.

"As has been observed, actions furnish the basis of determination of fitness for further service. What better guarantee of cordial and sound industrial relations between employee and employer than legislation which follows the lines of the Ohio workmen's compensation law? Under its influence, industrial conditions have improved, life and limb have been conserved, the workmen's families are happy in their security and a new era has dawned for millions of people. It was enacted when legislation of this sort was an experiment in America. If every state in this Union had a law of this sort our nation would have solved half of its industrial problems. Our courts are free from the vexatious litigation that fosters criticism and they are trusted as never before in history. It has been a factor of no small importance that enabled our state to uphold the sovereignty of the law without repressive measures directed against freedom of speech and pen.

"Educational activities have been quickened and rural life has been regenerated through modem school legislation. To the boys and girls of our rural districts there are coming schools which will be second to none in our most progressive cities, and one of the reasons for draining of the country districts of population will be checked. It has given an impetus to church and community life that is of greatest importance.

"These things are cited not because there is any disposition to urge that there should be encroachment by the federal government on local control. It is the healthful, reasonable individualism of American national life that has enabled the people of this country to think for themselves. We have no will to impair their independence. The central government can assist and give encouragement to state movements if the men called to high positions are in sympathy with progress. A reactionary central government can demonstrate likewise that it has no sympathy with men of vision who ever have difficult tasks in bringing about the taking of forward steps.

"The details of these instances, which might be greatly expanded, have been touched in order to form a setting as for a picture. Our view is toward tomorrow. The opposition, and I assume that they are sincere in it, stands in the skyline of the setting sun, looking backward, backward to the old days of reaction."

CHAPTER IV

COX AND THE LEAGUE—"I FAVOR GOING IN"

"And I do earnestly urge that all the people of this great and enlightened state assemble at their respective places of worship and invoke Almighty God to enlighten the Rulers of the world to the end that they may see the folly of war and speedily terminate it; that in our homes and about our hearthstones we implore the Divine Spirit in behalf of the people of the stricken nations, whose miseries are beyond our comprehension— people who have been plunged into the depths of war through no fault of their own.

"And I do further recommend and urge that in all the schools of the State of Ohio the afternoon of Friday, October 2nd, 1914, be set aside for exercises, having for their purpose to instill into the minds of children and into their hearts the great blessing that will come to them and to the world when war is no more."

The quoted sentences from Governor Cox's proclamation for a day of prayer on October 4, 1914, a period at which the horrors of the great world war had but begun, disclose that Governor Cox is not a recent convert to the central thought and purpose of the conception of the League of Nations.

Through the numerous official proclamations and the many addresses which he made during the period of the war the central thought repeatedly emphasized was that the fruit of war must be an everlasting peace. In accordance with the proclamation of the President, establishing June 5, 1917, as the "call-to-the- colors" day of the young men of the Country, the Governor said:

"It is probably the most trying hour the world has ever known, and the policies of government, purified and preserved by those who live now, will determine the civilization under which our children and our children's children shall live in the future. What greater guarantee of their peace and happiness can be given them than a democracy that envelops all nations—a democracy sanctified by an endearing memory of what was unselfishly given to make it possible?"

In his proclamation calling for a State convention to perfect the organization of an Ohio branch of the League to Enforce Peace, the Governor emphasized as the second of its objects "to keep the world safe by a League of Nations," and he said that the purpose of the organization would be "to confirm opposition to a premature peace and sustain the determination of our people to fight until Prussian militarism is destroyed and the way may be open for securing permanent peace by a League of Nations." When hostilities were concluded Governor Cox had the faith that "this peace brings the dawn of a new day of consecration," and in his official proclamation he said: "A world is reborn. Our Nation has brought success to a righteous cause. Our State has given with full heart to the achievement of the glorious end."

In an address in Toronto, Canada, November, 1918, Governor Cox said: "We consign to posterity an example and inspiration and idealism as lofty as ever stirred the hearts of men. And then, turning away from the past, we face the sunrise of to-morrow with faith and resolution to make a better world than that of yesterday, and to demonstrate that our heroic defenders have not died in vain. These are dangerous times to permit the inventive genius of man to go unchecked in matters of armament. The unspeakable horrors of the war just ended make us instinctively turn our faces away from the possibility of a half-century from now, if our thought is to be turned intensively to the production of things destructive to home life. With the sea fairly alive with submarines, the air filled with squadrons of flying machines, and the mysteries of nature unfolding before the sustained labor of chemists—cities and states and nations could be quickly depopulated. The Prussian conspiracy would not have been possible if the international affairs of the earth had been assigned to a League of Nations. The play may seem to be altruistic, if not fantastic, but the skeptic is moved by the idea that nations cannot forget selfishness. If that be true, then the world lacks the fundamental fibers of character to build an enduring civilization."

In welcoming the returned soldiers of the 166th Infantry in New York in may, 1919, Governor Cox said: "If peace is to endure, it must be by means of institutions of government whose strength in the right must inspire public confidence. We solemnly give the pledge of our state that the faith will be kept."

Economic effects of the defeat of the Treaty of Peace were discussed by Governor Cox at Henderson, Kentucky, in April, 1920. He said: "Some of you may not know the effect of the defeat of the Treaty. While at Mayfield (Ky.) I saw an old farmer who told me he was offered twenty and ten dollars for his tobacco before Christmas, but was forced to sell at six and three dollars. The tumbling of the foreign exchange and the inability of Italy and other Continental European countries to purchase their tobacco is the cause of Western Kentucky farmers losing millions of dollars. This resulted from the Republican Senate's refusal to ratify the peace treaty. While the

Republican dictators of the Senate set the stage for political triumph, they do not care how much tobacco growers or the people at large suffer.

Turning to the patriotic issue of the present campaign, he said at the same time: "It will be with infinite pleasure that we shall ask the Republican spellbinders if they have kept the faith with the boys who sleep overseas."

During all the progress of the early part of the campaign the Governor denounced those who "are seeking to set up racial lines and create a prejudice among the foreign elements in our midst." He said: "While other powers are doing everything possible to hold the loose ends of civilization together, these leaders are deliberately conspiring to mislead the great bulk of Americans with assertions that are, when analyzed, nothing more than demagoguery of the crudest kind." Earlier in the year, in speaking before the Jefferson Club of Marion, Indiana, the Governor said: "The plot to multiply the woes of mankind, in order that confusion multiplied might be charged to President Wilson's insistence on principle and international good faith, is now passing through the process of public thought, and we have confidence in an intelligent verdict. The winning of the war, in less time than the formalizing of peace carries a contrast that needs no comment."

During the period for the selection of delegates to the Democratic Convention at San Francisco, Governor Cox gave a signed interview to the New York Times, in which he reviewed the controversy concerning the League of Nations and outlined two reservations which he believed would satisfy every reasonable objection. In part, he said:

"If public opinion in the country is the same as it is in Ohio, then there can be no doubt but that the people want a League of Nations because it seems to offer the surest guarantee against war. I am convinced that the San Francisco Convention will endorse in its vital principles the League adopted at Versailles.

"There can be no doubt but that some senators have been conscientious in their desire to clarify the provisions of the treaty. Two things apparently have disturbed them. First, they wanted to make sure that the League was not to be an alliance, and that its basic purpose was peace and not controversy. Second, they wanted the other powers signing the instrument to understand our constitutional limitations beyond which the treaty-making power cannot go.

"Dealing with these two questions in order, it has always seemed to me that the interpretation of the function of the League might have been stated in these words:

"'In giving its assent to this treaty, the Senate has in mind the fact that the League of Nations which it embodies was devised for the sole purpose of maintaining peace and comity among the nations of the earth and preventing the recurrence of such destructive conflicts as that through which the world has just passed. The co-operation of the United States with the League and its continuance as a member thereof, will naturally depend upon the adherence of the League to that fundamental purpose.'

"Such a declaration would at least express the view of the United States and justify the course which our nation would unquestionably follow if the basic purpose of the League were at any time distorted. It would also appear to be a simple matter to provide against any misunderstanding in the future and at the same time to meet the objections of those who believe that we might be inviting a controversy over our constitutional rights, by making a senatorial addition on words something like these:

"'It will of course be understood that in carrying out the purpose of the League, the government of the United States must at all times act in strict harmony with the terms and intent of the United States Constitution, which cannot in any way be altered by the treaty-making power.'

"Some people doubt the enduring quality of this general international scheme. Whether this be true or not, the fact remains that it will justify itself if it does no more than prevent the nations of the earth from arming themselves to the teeth and wasting resource which is necessary to repair the losses of the war. No one contends that it is a perfect document, but it is a step in the right direction. It would put the loose ends of civilization together now and do more toward the restoration of normal conditions in six months' time than can the powers of the earth, acting independently, in ten years' time. The Republican senatorial cabal insists that the treaty be Americanized. Suppose that Italy asked that it be Italianized— France that it be Frenchized—Britain that it be Britainized, and so on down the line. The whole thing would result in a perfect travesty.

"The important thing now is to enable the world to go to work, but the beginning must not be on the soft sands of an unsound plan. If this question passes to the next administration, there should be no fetich developed over past differences. Yet at the same time there must be no surrender of vital principles. It may be necessary if partitions and reparation require changing, to assemble representatives of the people making up the nations of the League, in which event revision may not be so much an affair of diplomats. But I repeat the pressing task is getting started, being careful however that we are starting with an instrument worth while, and not a mere shadow."

To an extent to which very few public men favoring the League of Nations have gone, Governor Cox has expressed the firm conviction that the League will enable the people of Ireland to bring their contention and claims before a world tribunal. It was his statement before an audience in Cincinnati that the League would be the means by which the Irish case could be heard in the highest court in the world, and he stated that thus far it had never been heard even in a magistrate's court. Sentiments on the question of self-determination were also expressed in his article in the New York Times. In this the Governor said:

"We are a composite people in the United States and the belief of students of government in years past that our democracy would not endure was based entirely upon the idea that we could not build a nation from the blood of many races which had old inherited prejudices. It is very important, particularly at this time when racial impulses and emotions have been stirred world- wide as never before, that we make the utmost effort to prevent division along these lines. In this connection it is well to bear in mind that the armistice which preceded the peace was based upon fourteen cardinal points; one of the most, if not the most, important of which was the right of self-determination.

"Wars in the past have resulted largely from dispute over territory and imposed restraints of racial aspirations. Governmental entities are more apt to last and to live harmoniously with others if groups are bounded by racial homogeneity rather than by the physical characteristics of the earth in the form of mountains, rivers, etc. Individual aspiration is a God-given element and distinct ambitions possess the soul of racial unity. In harmony with this theory, the San Francisco convention should emphasize the Democratic belief in the principle of self-determination in government. Our citizens will not deny to any race of people the right to hold the emotions which stirred the founders of our Republic."

The Governor's position on the League was amplified in his Address of Acceptance at Dayton on August 7th, 1920, in which he said:

"We are in a time which calls for straight thinking, straight talking and straight acting. This is no time for wobbling. Never in all our history has more been done for government. Never was sacrifice more sublime. The most precious things of heart and home were given up in a spirit which guarantees the perpetuity of our institutions—if the faith is kept with those who served and suffered. The altar of our republic is drenched in blood and tears, and he who turns away from the tragedies and obligations of the war, not consecrated to a sense of honor and of duty which resists every base suggestion of personal or political expediency, is unworthy of the esteem of his countrymen.

"The men and women who by expressed policy at the San Francisco Convention charted our course in the open seas of the future sensed the spirit of the hour and phrased it with clarity and courage. It is not necessary to read and reread the Democratic platform to know its meaning. It is a document clear in its analysis of conditions and plain in the pledge of service made to the public. It carries honesty of word and intent. Proud of the leadership and achievement of the party in war, Democracy faces unafraid the problems of peace. Indeed, its pronouncement has but to be read along with the platform framed by Republican leaders in order that both spirit and purpose as they dominate the opposing organizations may be contrasted. On the one hand we see pride expressed in the nation's glory and a promise of service easily understood. On the other a captious, unhappy spirit and the treatment of subjects vital to the present and the future, in terms that have completely confused the public mind. It was clear that the senatorial oligarchy had been given its own way in the selection of the presidential candidate, but it was surprising that it was able to fasten into the party platform the creed of hate and bitterness and the vacillating policy that possesses it.

"In the midst of war the present senatorial cabal, led by Senators Lodge, Penrose and Smoot, was formed. Superficial evidence of loyalty to the President was deliberate in order that the great rank and file of their party, faithful and patriotic to the very core, might not be offended. But underneath this misleading exterior, conspirators planned and plotted, with bigoted zeal. With victory to our arms they delayed and obstructed the works of peace. If deemed useful to the work in hand no artifice for interfering with our constitutional peace-making authority was rejected. Before the country knew, yes, before these men themselves knew the details of the composite plan, formed at the peace table, they declared their opposition to it. Before the treaty was submitted to the senate in the manner the Constitution provides, they violated every custom and every consideration of decency by presenting a copy of the document, procured unblushingly from enemy hands, and passed it into the printed record of senatorial proceedings. From that hour dated the enterprise of throwing the whole subject into a technical discussion, in order that the public might be confused. The plan has never changed in its objective, but the method has. At the outset there was the careful insistence that there was no desire to interfere with the principle evolved and formalized at Versailles. Later, it was the form and not the substance that professedly inspired attack. But pretense was futile when proposals later came forth that clearly emasculated the basic principle of the whole peace plan. It is not necessary to recall the details of the controversy in the senate. Senator Lodge finally crystallized his ideas into what were known as the Lodge reservations, and when congress adjourned these reservations held the support of the so-called regular Republican leaders.

"From that time the processes have been interesting. Political expediency in its truest sense dwarfed every consideration either of the public interest or of the maintenance of the honor of a great political party. The exclusive question was how to avoid a rupture in the Republican organization. The country received with interest, to say the least, the announcement from Chicago, where the national convention was assembled, that a platform plank dealing with the subject of world peace, had been drawn leaving out the Lodge reservations, and yet remaining agreeable to all interests, meaning thereby, the Lodge reservationists, the mild reservationists and the group of Republican senators that openly opposed the League of Nations in any form.

"As the platform made no definite committal of policy and was, in fact, so artfully phrased as to make almost any deduction possible, it passed through the convention with practical unanimity. Senator Johnson, however, whose position has been consistent and whose opposition to the League in any shape is well known, withheld his support of the convention's choice until the candidate had stated the meaning of the platform, and announced definitely the policy that would be his, if elected.

"The Republican candidate has spoken and his utterance calls forth the following approval from Senator Johnson:

"'Yesterday in his speech of acceptance Senator Harding unequivocally took his stand upon the paramount issue in this campaign—the League of Nations. The Republican party stands committed by its platform. Its standard-bearer has now accentuated that platform. There can be no misunderstanding his words.'

"Senator Harding, as the candidate of the party, and Senator Johnson are as one on this question, and, as the latter expresses it, the Republican party is committed both by platform in the abstract and by its candidate in specification. The threatened revolt among leaders of the party is averted, but the minority position as expressed in the senate prevails as that of the party. In short, principle, as avowed in support of the Lodge reservations, or of the so-called mild reservations, has been surrendered to expediency.

"Senator Harding makes this new pledge of policy in behalf of his party:

"'I promise you formal and effective peace so quickly as a Republican congress can pass its declaration for a Republican executive to sign.'

"This means but one thing—a separate peace with Germany!

"This would be the most disheartening event in civilization since the Russians made their separate peace with Germany, and infinitely more unworthy on our part than it was on that of the Russians. They were threatened with starvation and revolution had swept their country. Our soldiers fought side by side with the Allies. So complete was the coalition of strength and purpose that General Fochs was given supreme command, and every soldier in the allied cause, no matter what flag he followed, recognized him as his chief. We fought the war together, and now before the thing is through it is proposed to enter into a separate peace with Germany! In good faith we pledged our strength with our associates for the enforcement of terms upon offending powers, and now it is suggested that this be withdrawn. Suppose Germany, recognizing the first break in the Allies, proposes something we cannot accept. Does Senator Harding intend to send an army to Germany to press her to our terms? Certainly the allied army could not be expected to render aid. If, on the other hand, Germany should accept the chance we offered of breaking the bond it would be for the express purpose of insuring a German-American alliance, recognizing that the Allies—in fact, no nation in good standing—would have anything to do with either of us.

"This plan would not only be a piece of bungling diplomacy, but plain, unadulterated dishonesty, as well."

"No less an authority than Senator Lodge said, before the heat of recent controversy, that to make peace except in company with the Allies would 'brand us everlastingly with dishonor and bring ruin to us.'

"And then after peace is made with Germany, Senator Harding would, he says, 'hopefully approach the nations of Europe and of the earth, proposing that understanding which makes us a willing participant in the consecration of nations to a new relationship.'

"In short, America, refusing to enter the League of Nations (now already established by twenty-nine nations) and bearing and deserving the contempt of the world, would submit an entirely new project. This act would either be regarded as arrant madness or attempted international bossism.

"The plain truth is, that the Republican leaders, obsessed with a determination to win the presidential election, have attempted to satisfy too many divergent views. Inconsistencies, inevitable under the circumstances, rise to haunt them on every hand, and they find themselves arrayed, in public thought at least, against a great principle. More than that, their conduct is opposed to the idealism upon which their party prospered in other days."

"Illustrating these observations by concrete facts, let it be remembered that those now inveighing against an interest in affairs outside of America, criticised President Wilson in unmeasured terms for not resenting the invasion of Belgium in 1914. They term the League of Nations a military alliance, which, except for their opposition, would envelop our country, when, as a matter of truth, the subject of a League of Nations has claimed the best thought of America for years, and the League to Enforce Peace was presided over by so distinguished a Republican as ex-President Taft, who, before audiences in every section, advocated the principle and the plan of the present League. They charge experimentation, when we have as historical precedent the Monroe Doctrine, which is the very essence of Article X of the Versailles covenant. Skeptics viewed Monroe's mandate with alarm, predicting recurrent wars in defense of Central and South American states, whose guardians they alleged we need not be. And yet not a shot has been fired in almost one hundred years in preserving sovereign rights on this hemisphere. They hypocritically claim that the League of Nations will result in our boys being drawn into military service, but they fail to realize that every high-school youngster in the land knows that no treaty can override our Constitution, which reserves to Congress, and to Congress alone, the power to declare war. They preach Americanism with a meaning of their own invention, and artfully appeal to a selfish and provincial spirit, forgetting that Lincoln fought a war over the purely moral question of slavery, and the McKinley broke the fetters of our boundary lines, spoke the freedom of Cuba, and carried the torch of American idealism to the benighted Philippines. They lose memory of Garfield's prophecy that America, under the blessings of God- given opportunity, would by her moral leadership and co- operation become the Messiah among the nations of the earth.

"These are fateful times. Organized government has a definite duty all over the world. The house of civilization is to be put in order. The supreme issue of the century is before us and the nation that halts and delays is playing with fire. The finest impulses of humanity, rising above national lines, merely seek to make another horrible war impossible. Under the old order of international anarchy war came overnight, and the world was on fire before we knew it. It sickens our senses to think of another. We saw one conflict into which modern science brought new forms of destruction in great guns, submarines, airships, and poison gases. It is no secret that our chemists had perfected, when the contest came to a precipitate close, gases so deadly that whole cities could be wiped out, armies destroyed, and the crews of battleships smothered. The public prints are filled with the opinions of military men that in future wars the method, more effective than gases or bombs, will be the employment of the germs of disease, carrying pestilence and destruction. Any nation prepared under these conditions, as Germany was equipped in 1914, could conquer the world in a year.

"It is planned now to make this impossible. A definite plan has been agreed upon. The League of Nations is in operation. A very important work, under its control, just completed, was participated in by the Hon. Elihu Root, Secretary of State under the Roosevelt administration. At a meeting of the Council of the League of Nations, February 11, and organizing committee of twelve of the most eminent jurists in the world was selected. The duty of this group was to devise a plan for the establishment of a Permanent Court of International Justice, as a branch of the League. This assignment has been concluded by unanimous action. This augurs well for world progress. The question is whether we shall or shall not join in this practical and humane movement. President Wilson, as our representative at the peace table, entered the League in our name, in so far as the executive authority permitted. Senator Harding, as the Republican candidate for the presidency, proposes in plain words that we remain out of it. As the Democratic candidate, I favor going in. Let us analyze Senator Harding's plan of making a German-American peace, and then calling for a 'new relationship among nations,' assuming for the purpose of argument only, that the perfidious hand that dealt with Germany would possess the power or influence to draw twenty-nine nations away from a plan already at work, and induce them to retrace every step and make a new beginning. This would entail our appointing another commission to assemble with those selected by the other powers. With the Versailles instrument discarded, the whole subject of partitions and divisions of territory on new lines would be reopened. The difficulties in this regard, as any fair mind appreciates, would be greater than they were at the peace session, and we must not attempt to convince ourselves that they did not try the genius, patience, and diplomacy of statesmen at that time. History will say that great as was the Allied triumph in war, no less a victory was achieved at the peace table. The Republican proposal means dishonor, world confusion and delay. It would keep us in permanent company with Germany, Russia, Turkey and Mexico. It would entail, in the ultimate, more real injury than the war itself. The Democratic position on the question, as expressed in platform is:

"'We advocate immediate ratification of the Treaty without reservations which would impair its essential integrity, but do no oppose the acceptance of any reservation making clearer or more specific the obligations of the United States to the League associates.'

"The first duty of the new administration clearly will be the ratification of the Treaty. The matter should be approached without thought of the bitterness of the past. The public verdict will have been rendered, and I am confident that the friends of world peace as it will be promoted by the League, will have in numbers the constitutional requisite to favorable senatorial action. The captious may say that our platform reference to reservations is vague and indefinite. Its meaning, in brief, is that we shall state our interpretation of the covenant as a matter of good faith to our associates and as a precaution against any misunderstanding in the future. The point is, that after the people shall have spoken, the League will be in the hands of its friends in the Senate, and a safe index as to what they will do is supplied by what reservations they have proposed in the past.

"Our platform clearly lays no bar against any additions that will be helpful, but it speaks in a firm resolution to stand against anything that disturbs the vital principle. We hear it said that interpretations are unnecessary. That may be true, but they will at least be reassuring to many of our citizens, who feel that in signing the treaty, there should be no mental reservations that are not expressed in plain words, as a matter of good faith to our associates. Such interpretations possess the further virtue of supplying a base upon which agreement can be reached, and agreement, without injury to the covenant, is now of pressing importance. It was the desire to get things started, that prompted some members of the senate to vote for the Lodge reservations. Those who conscientiously voted for them in the final roll calls realized, however, that they acted under duress, in that a politically bigoted minority was exercising the arbitrary power of its position to enforce drastic conditions. Happily the voters of the republic, under our system of government, can remedy that situation, and I have the faith that they will, at the election this fall. Then organized government will be enabled to combine impulse and facility in the making of better world conditions. The agencies of exchange will automatically adjust themselves to the opportunities of commercial freedom. New life and renewed hope will take hold of every nation. Mankind will press a resolute shoulder to the task of readjustment, and a new era will have dawned upon the earth."

Speaking to the National Guardsmen at the National Rifle Matches at Camp Perry, Ohio, on August 12, he said:

"I recognize that in a sense you are assembled here for the purpose of increasing the efficiency of our military strength, and yet I am convinced that the great mass of our soldiers are united in purpose and prayer, to prevent wars in the future, if it can be honorably done. They know the meaning of modern warfare. There was very little romance in the long hours and the slaughter of the front trench. The thought that must have run through the mind of every solder in the midst of it all, was how such a thing was possible in modern civilization.

"The cost to the United States was more than one million dollars an hour for over two years. The total expense of twenty-two billion dollars was almost equal to the total disbursements of the United States government from 1791 to 1918. It was sufficient to have run the Revolutionary War for more than one thousand years at the rate of expenditure which that war involved. The army expenditures alone, so experts claim, are a near approach to the volume of gold produced in the United Sates from the discovery of America up to the outbreak of the European War, and yet the United States spent only about one-eighth of the entire cost of the war, and less than one-fifth of the expenditure of the allied side.

"If civilization has not had its lesson, then there is no hope for it. It could not stand such a war again and survive. The genius of man, if that is a happy term in discussing the horrors of conflict, has always made the latest war the most frightful. When we consider the development in the methods of human destruction between 1914 and 1918 and apply the problem of simple proportion, we are staggered even to think of the possibilities of the sons of men being again brought into combat.

"There will always be a national guard in the States, if for no other reason than domestic defense, and the military arm of the federal government will be maintained, but the hope that vast expenditures for armaments are a thing of the past, possesses every home in America, while the common impulse that moves the great mass of people world-wide is inspired by the vision of peace and the settlement of controversy by the arbitrament of reason rather than of force."

At the very beginning of his canvass for the Presidency Governor Cox has gone upon the theory that the League of Nations needed simple explanation to the people of the Country. In his own phrase, he has talked the ABC's of the League, finding that the technical discussions had failed to hold the interest of the people. Illustrating this policy are two addresses made to state conventions early in August. At Wheeling, to the West Virginia Democratic Convention, he said:

"We resisted a world-wide menace, and we intend now to establish permanent protection against another menace. We know how easily wars came in the past. We want to make their coming difficult in the future. We have a definite plan; the American people understand it, and after the 4th of March, 1921, it is our purpose to put it into practical operation, without continuing months of useless discussion.

"The platform of our party gives us the opportunity to render moral co-operation in the greatest movement of righteousness in the history of the world, and at the same time to hold our own interests free from peril. Our position is plain. The circumstances of the last eighteen months convict the Republican leadership of attempted trickery with the American people. Under one pretext after another they prevented the readjustment of national conditions. They proposed certain reservations to the League of Nations, and then they were abandoned, to be followed by nothing more definite than the announcement of a 'hope' that an entirely new arrangement might be made in world affairs. What method they have in mind, if it is concretely in anyone's mind, the people do not know. No unprejudiced person can deny that the consequence of abandoning the League and attempting an entirely new project, will be prolonged delay. If the voters of the Republic, without regard to party, desire action, and prompt action along lines that are now clearly understood, they will render a verdict so overwhelmingly expressive of public indignation that scheming politicians for years to come will not forget.

"In the fact of an efficient leadership during the war, and of constructive, progressive, economic service in peace, the Republican leaders developed a smoke screen, behind which they seek to gain their objective, the spoils of office. For years the best thought and the humanitarian impulses of civilized countries have been applied to the high purpose of making war practically impossible. The League of Nations became the composite agreement, and now the senatorial oligarchy meets it with the absurd plea that it increases the probability of armed conflict. It not only reveals unworthy intent, but a very poor estimate of American intelligence as well."

Taking the issue to the people, and free from what he termed strait-jacket restrictions, the Governor said at Columbus, when he talked to the Ohio Democratic Convention:

"I carefully reviewed the platform adopted at Chicago, and studied its principles, but I know as much about it now as when I started to read it. I gave intensive thought also to the speech made by the Republican candidate, the purpose of which was to interpret the meaning of that historic document, and after long and vigilant labor I found two pronouncements. What was the first? The statement that staggered the sensibilities of the civilization of the world, the unthinkable, monstrous proposal, that in the midst of the uncertainty of the hour, a separate peace ought to be made with Germany. I want you to go back with me just a year and a half, to the time when victory was son; to the time when our boys maintained their vigils on the banks of the Rhine, standing there in solid formation with 2,000,000 great lads behind them. Germany signed the peace document on the dotted line. What has happened in the united States Senate to prevent its acceptance by the upper branch of the American Congress? I need not recall, because every child knows about it. But the soldiers came back home; they were demobilized; they entered into their several walks of life believing that their victory had been complete, and that the offending powers had been brought to terms. And now, with the armies disbanded, and now, with our military strength no longer holding together, it is proposed by the candidate of the Republican party that he will prove false to the boys who stood by when that peace was made. He will destroy the pact and enter into a new covenant.

"Six hundred thousand French died at Verdun defending the slogan, 'They shall not pass.' More than a million English and Canadians died on the Somme, reforming their ranks, and hurling back the challenge, 'They shall not pass.' They were possessed of the crusading spirit; they were preserving the Democracy of the world, the very Government of the earth. And now another menace is threatened, and it is proposed that some one, acting in behalf of two millions of soldiers and the one hundred million people of this Republic, shall perform a perfectly perfidious act. Standing at the head of the hosts of the great army which opposes the hosts of reaction; standing at the head of the hosts of Democracy, at the head of the hosts of progress; at the head of the hundreds of thousands of independents of this Country, I give to you this assurance: That this dishonorable deed will not be perpetrated—for two very important reasons. First, Warren G. Harding will not have a chance to do it; and second, I will not insult two million soldiers by doing it myself.

"And then proceeding to the second stage of these proceedings, the Republican candidate says that after he shall have made a separate peace with Germany, he will then assemble the conscience of the civilization of the world and form an entirely new relationship. If, for the sake of argument only, we are to assume that a separate peace with Germany were made, I believe that the Government of the United States of America would be so unworthy in the eyes of the nations of the world that none of them would have anything to do with us at all.

"This one question will remain in the public mind. After all this is the crux of the whole situation. The Republican candidate and the reactionaries now in control of the Republican party, promise you nothing whatsoever except a proposal which at is best will involve months and probably years of delay. On the other hand, we promise you this, that after the 4th of March, 1921, with the least amount of conversation possible, we will enter the League of Nations of the world. Our Democratic platform adopted at San Francisco gives us full license and opportunity to enter the League upon terms which will need no defense. Our position is not unbending; it is not captious. We proclaim that we will accept any conditions that interpret, that call attention to the limitations of our Constitution; that serve full notice now upon the powers of the earth that we can go so far and no further.

"In other words we have the opportunity of concluding this, the greatest movement for righteousness in all the history of the world, and then the loose ends of civilization will be put together. The opportunity for exchange will have been restored. America will proceed upon an era of prosperity and peace without precedent.

"I shall address no audience in America this year without puncturing the smoke screen of hypocrisy and insincerity which has been raised, in order that the reactionaries might creep in behind it and claim their main objective, the spoils of office. That smoke screen now is the statement that the League of Nations increases the probabilities of war. It would have been just as absurd to have said to the boys at the time our fathers won their freedom, that if you proclaim your independence you are going to have war, because you will have to fight to retain it. Every school boy in Ohio understands there are three branches of Government, Judicial, Legislative and Executive, and when war has been brought to an end, the head of the Executive Department, the President of the United States, makes the treaty with the power with which we have been at war, and then we find that limitation of power. The President can go no further. He submits it to the Senate for ratification. The President of the United States has very definite power, and there are also very specific powers reserved to the Congress of the United States. The Congress can do nothing contrary to the Constitution; the President can do nothing contrary to the Constitution. The Constitution provides that war can be declared by Congress, and Congress only. In order to give point and truth to what the reactionary leaders are now contending for, it would be necessary to change the Constitution of the United States. This would require a two-thirds' vote of the House and Senate, and then a three-fourths' vote of the states of the Union. Our machinery was so adjusted that no matter who might be the Executive Officer of this Republic, he did not possess the power to declare war. The power was placed as near to the people as it was possible to place it. It was placed with their Representatives in Congress.

"Now—the Republican leaders in contending that four or five potentates, four or five distinguished statesmen over seas, sitting in the council of the League of Nations, can order our soldiers anywhere, are speaking a deliberate and a willful untruth. Presidential proprieties require that I do not characterize it in stronger language. You know it is very hard to please the opposition, although we are under great debt to them for having made the gauge of battle in this campaign. The proposition to disgrace America by making a separate peace with Germany was simply opening their front lines. I have already entered that opening with the hosts of Democracy around me.

"About three months ago a well-meaning Republican business man was driving through Clark county. His soldier boy was at the wheel, and he looked over into a field and saw a hundred trucks lying there; and he seized upon the circumstance to attack the Administration at Washington. The son had heard enough of it, and he stopped the car and said: 'Father, you have got to stop talking that way. When we were in the front trench we had warm food, no matter whether we were in the midst of hell's fire or not. We had all the ammunition we needed. It was ten times better to have more trucks than we needed than to have fewer trucks than we needed.' And then there is another reason for it all. Need we be reminded that the opposition said that it would require Secretary Baker and President Wilson eighteen months to take 600,000 soldiers over seas, and, recognizing that it would require in all probability more than 2,000,000 soldiers to win the war, that the war would then last, under this Democratic Administration, four times eighteen months. Any child in this country can have the facts presented to him and he will have the mentality to grasp these outstanding circumstances: President Wilson and Secretary Baker, at the head of the military forces of the nation did not send 600,000 soldiers over in eighteen months' time. They sent 2,000,000 soldiers over in eighteen months' time, and won the war without the loss of a single troop ship."

CHAPTER V

HOW HE HAS DEALT WITH LABOR TROUBLES

No subject furnishes so good an index to the entire record of an executive as the manner in which he has handled the affairs growing out of industrial disputes. Touching, as they often do, a zone of disputed claims, and involving, as they often do, the social rights of workers no less than the rights of property, and entailing, as they frequently have, the duty of maintaining public order, the conflicts between capital and labor test to the utmost the abilities of the Executive Officer of a great industrial state like Ohio. Within its borders are toilers from every land and every clime. In her cities dwell as laborers men and women from every known country and representative of every race—a modern Babel of tongues with a greater variety, were it possible, than those upon whom fell confusion of speech in the ages gone.

And the period during which Governor Cox has held away has been one of profound upheavals. There have been strikes brought forth by "hard times," strikes occasioned by efforts at organization of workers, and strikes whose distant origin lay in the economic overturn incident to war inflation with its topsy-turvy of values and its jumble of the normal status. These conditions, then, supply a complete and ample test of the effectiveness of the policy which has been followed. The results of this policy are told in a brief statement by Mr. Oscar W. Newman, Associate Justice of the Ohio Supreme Court. He said: "Not a soldier was brought to the scene of a single strike (although they were in readiness for emergency); person and property were preserved; and above all, the dignity of the law was maintained."

Nor has capital been offended by the methods pursued. This fact is attested by statements of those who speak for invested industrial wealth. Thus, W. S. Thomas, of Springfield, says that the policies pursued have made "Ohio an oasis in the widespread area of industrial turmoil during and since the great war."

There are cited, too, the conclusions reached by Thomas J. Donnelly, Secretary of the Ohio Federation of labor, who has written:

"Labor has confidence in James M. Cox because the laboring people feel that he understands their needs and is in hearty sympathy with the progressive aspirations of those who earn their bread by the sweat of their brows. As governor, he accomplished more in the interest of the laboring people of Ohio and is held in higher esteem by them than any other governor in the state's history.

"He has done much to avoid and to settle labor troubles. He believes that more can be accomplished through reason and common sense than through force and intimidation; and whenever called upon to send the militia to deal with striking workmen, he always found a way to prevent violence and preserve order without using soldiers for that purpose. During the big steel strike when violence and disorder were rampant in some states where the right peaceably to assemble had been denied to the striking workers, in Ohio, where there were equally as many strikers involved, there was no sign of violence, and the right of workers peaceably to assembled was not interfered with. If his policy had been followed by other public officials throughout the nation, there would be less unrest and the people would have more confidence in the fairness of government authorities."

It is only necessary to get a comprehensive view of Governor Cox's record with respect to labor troubles to tell the plain story of what he has done. He had scarce taken hold as Governor in 1913 when a strike broke out in the great rubber plants of Akron. It seemed to have been fomented by members of the Industrial Workers of the World, but it drew in its train thousands upon thousands of other workers until the great plants were practically idle. In Akron, where a heterogenous collection of industrial workers dwell, idleness was a potent factor in fomenting disorder. The normal course of affairs would have been an attempt to operate the plants with strike breakers under guard, provocative acts upon both sides, and finally, recourse to an armed militia to quell the disorder after the inevitable bloodshed had ensued. Although new in executive experience, Governor Cox took another course. He sent trained and trusted investigators to Akron who learned the facts and reported to him accurately upon the situation, including also the grievances of the toilers. At the same time he gave warning to the local authorities that they preserve a strict neutrality in their dealing with the contending forces, and he uttered a solemn warning that the laws must be respected, assuring those of both contending factions that public opinion within the city would speedily ascertain the right and wrong of the controversy. And so it proved to be. But learning there were abuses in the plants that needed correction the Governor gave his assent to an investigation by a legislative committee through the helpful publicity of which all interests were induced to redress certain grievances. It gave an object lesson not only to Akron but to all the state. It taught even the turbulent element that only harm could come through infraction of the law and through disrespect for rights of person and property. The remainder of the story is that I. W. W. disturbers have more sterile soil in Ohio to cultivate than in any of the states about it.

A startling comparison two years later at East Youngstown, during the administration of Governor Cox's successor, disclosed by contrast the value of the peaceful plan. Through a policy of uncertainty and wavering, a riot was allowed to start and military were needed to put down the disorder, life being lost in the process.

The details of the incidents of similar nature to that of Akron need not be recounted here, but the invariable policy pursued was the collection of all the facts, so far as possible, by a representative of capital and one of labor. Of this course, the simple statement can be made that it was eminently successful.

This recital has been made as a preliminary to the narrative of the great steel strike of 1919 on which the Governor's fame as an administrator in troubled times largely rests. The same policy of investigation and research was pursued. Solemn warning was given that freedom of speech and assembly must be respected rigidly but that neither must become the instrument of license nor of subversive speech or conduct. At the time when the situation reached a critical stage the Governor issued this statement:

"To the Mayors of municipalities and County Sheriffs of Ohio:

"I am impressed with the importance of a statement to the mayors and sheriffs as to a policy which should serve as a guide to government, both state and local, in the matter of turbulent conditions which have developed in many communities, from pending industrial disputes.

"We have inquiry at the executive office from local officials clearly indicating that no rule of action has been developed in the face of present emergencies and further that none is in prospect. The constitution imposes upon the Governor the very definite responsibility of law enforcement. While it is the duty of the mayor of a municipality and the sheriff of the county to execute the laws, the founders of our charter of government gave to the state executive, not only the right to keep vigilant eye on conditions in every community, but his oath imposes the obligation so to do. Therefore, in no part of the state must a public officer permit the violation of the law. The mayors and sheriffs seem to have proper concept of their duty in the abstract. The purpose of this statement is to deal with specifications.

"The sections of the state which give the greatest concern have large masses of alien residents. Thousands of them do not speak the language. They are not familiar with our laws but it is safe to assume that the individual conscience tells every man that violence is both a moral and a legal wrong.

"Officers of companies whose manufacturing plants are closed by strike or other cause have expressed to me the intention to resume operations. At the same time they have asked for 'protection.' Inquiry develops this fact—that some employers believe it the duty of government to transport their employees into and out of the plants in question. This is not a function of government. Throughout the years, the policy has been not to make use of soldiers nor policemen to man street cars, for instance, nor in any way to make of them the instruments to bring a strike to an end. If either state or local officers provided safe conveyance of workmen into or out of a manufacturing institution, then government would be making of itself the agent of one of the parties to the dispute. If, however, the plant resumes, and disorder of any sort ensues as the result of employees going into or out of the factory, then that becomes an affair of governmental concern and the mayor of the municipality or the sheriff of the county, as location within or without the municipality largely determines, must suppress violence and arrest those who violate the law. I shall exact this from all local officers.

"Picketing as we understand it is neither prohibited by law nor condemned by public sentiment, but it must go no further than moral persuasion Organized society cannot continue without government, and government will not live unless the laws are respected. They not only express what experience has taught us, but they are the official mandate of the will of the majority, and after all, that is a fundamental principle in a republic.

"All officers must act with care. It will be found that trouble can often be avoided by an open, frank and firm contact of public officers with both the representatives of the employers and employees. No call that I have ever made upon either side of these controversies has ever gone unheeded.

"We are in the midst of unprecedented conditions, but if we devote ourselves to the single thought of making government the agency of justice and the instrument of bringing swift punishment to those who violate the laws of this commonwealth, we will pass through the storm safely.

"No man must be permitted to define the rules of his individual conduct. The law is supreme. I shall expect its enforcement by local officers. When they have rendered their utmost effort and failed to meet conditions, then the state will act promptly."

In every city in Ohio, save one, this warning was sufficient, but in Canton it became necessary for the Governor to remove the mayor. His successor speedily re-established the peace.

CHAPTER VI

HOW HE HAS DEALT WITH INDUSTRIAL RELATIONS

The story of the result of Governor Cox's treatment of industrial issues is told in his parallel of statements from Thomas J. Donnelly, Secretary of the Ohio Federation of Labor, and W. S. Thomas, a leading manufacturer.

Statement by Donnelly:

"Before Ohio had a Workmen's Compensation Law, only twenty per cent of the injured workers, or the widows and children of deceased workers, were paid any compensation or damages. Eighty per cent got nothing whatever. When Cox was first elected governor, about five per cent of the workers of Ohio were covered under an optional Workmen's Compensation Law. His first move as governor was to insist upon the passage of a Workmen's Compensation Law that would benefit all the workers. In this he met with powerful and bitter opposition. But through his determined efforts the opposition was overcome and the law was passed. To-day the Ohio State Insurance Fund is the largest carrier of workmen's compensation insurance, public or private, in the world. More than a million dollars a month is being collected by this fund, all of which is paid out for compensation and medical treatment for the injured workers or the dependents of those who are killed in the course of employment. This law supplied such an urgent need in the state that the employers and the laboring people of Ohio now look upon it as an accomplishment that outshines any other achievement in the state's history.

"The report of the legislative agents of the Ohio State Federation of Labor show that fifty-six laws in behalf of laboring people were passed during Cox's three terms as governor. Among these were laws forbidding the exploitation of women and children and limiting their hours of labor, providing for mothers' pensions, providing for safety codes to protect life, limb and health and numerous other beneficent measures."

Statement by Thomas:

"His strong sense of right and wrong, and the exercise of an unusual common sense, together with his frankness and courage in expression, have been the controlling factors in his successful relationship with the business interests of the state.

"A single example of his wisdom will illustrate this. For years organized labor and organized capital in Ohio have met during the sessions of the general assembly in what seemed to be a necessary antagonism. This was evidenced by the opposition of each to the proposed measures of the other. The result was ill feeling and little accomplished for either. It was Governor Cox's suggestion that these organizations, represented by the State Federation of Labor and the Ohio Manufacturers' Association, through their executive officers, should meet together and discuss pending legislation relating to the interest of either. Finally this plan was adopted, and it is the testimony of those participating tat it did much to avoid misunderstandings, and contributed a great deal towards sane and safe legislation. There is not known any instance of this plan being adopted in any other state of the Union. The fruit of this sensible procedure is that there are no laws in Ohio that hamper industry, impede business or endanger property interests, and at the same time the state is foremost in legislation that promotes social welfare, gives labor its due, and helps the weak and needy.

"A man who has occupied this position without interruption during three administrations would be a failure at the very outstart if he resorted to devious conduct or political duplicity. He has but one master—the people at large. To reach this position he had to have courage, be truthful, exercise sound and practical business judgment, and at the same time have a vision looking to the betterment of the condition of his fellow-man."

The cornerstone of the labor legislation is the Workmen's Compensation Law, the story of which is told in the state archives, in the messages to the Ohio General Assembly. At the beginning of his first term as Governor in 1913, Governor Cox said:

"It would certainly be common bad faith not to pass a compulsory Workmen's Compensation Law. No subject was discussed during the last campaign with greater elaboration, and it must be stated to the credit of our citizenship generally that regardless of the differences of opinion existing for many years, the justice of the compulsory feature is now admitted. Much of the criticism of the courts has been due to the trials of personal injury cases under the principles of practice which held the fellow-servant rule, and assumption of risk and contributory negligence to be grounds of defense. The layman reaches his conclusion with respect to justice along the lines of common sense, and the practice in personal injury cases has been so sharply in conflict with the plain fundamentals of right, that social unrest has been much contributed to. A second phase of this whole subject which has been noted in the development of the great industrialism of the day has been the inevitable animosity between capital and labor through the ceaseless litigation growing out of these cases. The individual or the corporation that employs on a large scale has taken insurance in liability companies, and, in too many instances, cases which admitted of little difference of opinion have been carried into the courts. The third injustice has been the waste occasioned by the system. The injured workman or the family deprived of its support by accident is not so circumstanced that the case can be contested with the corporation to the court of last resort. The need of funds compels compromise on a base that is not always equitable. Human nature many times drives sharp bargains that can hardly be endorsed by the moral scale. In the final analysis the cost of attorney fees is so heavy that the amount which finally accrues in cases of accident is seriously curtailed before it reaches the beneficiary. These three considerations clearly suggest the lifting of this whole operation out of the courts and the sphere of legal disputation. And then there is a broader principle which must be recognized. There is no characteristic of our civilization so marked as the element of interdependence as between social units. We are all dependent upon our fellows in one way or another. Some occupations, however, are more hazardous than others and the rule of the past in compelling those engaged in dangerous activities to bear unaided the burden of this great risk, is not right. The Workmen's Compensation Law in this state, which, however, lacks the compulsory feature, has made steady growth in popularity. The heavy decrease in rates clearly indicates economy and efficiency in the administration of the state liability board of awards. The compulsory feature, however, should at once be added. I respectfully but very earnestly urge its adoption amendatory of the present law with such other changes as experience might dictate.

"The objective to be sought is the fullest measure of protection to those engaged in dangerous occupations with the least burden of cost to society, because after all the social organization must pay for it. The ultimate result of this law will be the reduction in death and accident because not only the humanitarian but the commercial consideration will suggest the necessity of installing and maintaining with more vigilance modern safety devices.

"Government as a science must make its improvement along the same practical lines which develop system, simplification, classification of kindred activities, and better administrative direction in the evolution of business. A private or corporate enterprise is compelled to promote in the highest degree both efficiency and economy because its income is subject to the hazards of business. Government without this spur of necessity because its revenue is both regular and certain, does not effect reorganizations and combine common activities so readily. One reason, of course, is that new legislation is required and that is not easy at all times. Wherever human energies are now being directed toward more efficient public service, we find the consolidation under one administrative unit or bureau of all departments which deal either in direct or different manner with the same general subject. Investigation develops many duplications in both labor and expense in the departments of the state. No business institution would continue such a policy and recognizing now the importance of conducting the business of the commonwealth along the same modern and efficient lines of private and corporate operations, there is submitted herewith to your honorable body two recommendations which, in my judgment, are of tremendous importance, namely, the creation of an Industrial Commission and a Department of Agriculture. The first named organization would combine every existing department which deals with the relation between capital and labor. It is certainly a logical observation that the department heads clothed with the responsibility of details will find it extremely difficult to rise to the moral vision necessary to construct and conserve policies dealing with big things. Besides duplication of service is a waste of both human energy and state funds."

In summing up the results of a single year of Workmen's Compensation Law, the Governor at the beginning of 1915 said:

"The humane results of the Workmen's compensation Law have been so widespread and the wisdom of the people in changing the constitution so as to make this plan compulsory has been so completely demonstrated that manufacturer and employee now join in praise of the act. While the liability insurance companies contend that the State could not administer this trust and that the cost would run into millions of dollars per year, the experience of the first twelve months shows the cost of the administration to be approximately $160,000; and the claims, running far in excess of 50,000 in number, have been adjudicated with such promptness as to justify in the fullest measure the soundness of the State plan. The balance in the fund December 15, 1914, was $2,418,414.07. The number of accidents is diminishing and the cost to the employer is decreasing; so that both lower rates and larger compensation seem assured. As one who passed through the stormy period that led to the passage of this law, I urge upon you the extreme importance of the highest manifestations of vigilance, patriotism and humanity in order that the fundamentals of this beneficent legislation may be preserved. Under the pretext of improving the law it can be easily emasculated. Ohio assumed the lead in this legislation, and if the fundamental principle is maintained here, the plan, by its demonstrated worth, will be adopted elsewhere. This means the ultimate loss of ill-gotten millions by potential interests that have grown rich from the tears, blood and maimed bodies of our working people. They will not give it up without a continued struggle. Your duty to humanity and to your State calls for extreme watchfulness.

Though he suffered defeat for re-election in 1914, neither the Industrial Commission Law nor the Workmen's compensation Law nor any other major piece of social legislation was disturbed by his successor. In reviewing four years of the history of the law at his re-accession to power in 1917, he said:

"Since the adoption of the law there have been 300,000 industrial accidents and only seventeen suits have been brought against employers who paid into the state insurance fund. There was but one single verdict rendered by the court against the employer in the list of seventeen and that was for $2000. Five cases were settled out of court, four were decided in favor of the employer, one was dismissed by the employee, one was dismissed by the court and four are still pending. More than one thousand firms carry their own insurance under state consent, and against these institutions but five suits have been brought. Against the employers who have reinsured with the liability insurance companies, eight suits have been instituted, making a total of thirty law suits from all sources. These figures are procured from the official records of the Industrial Commission."

Two years later, in 1919, a further chapter is given:

"The experience of our state with the Compulsory Workmen's Compensation Law bears so vitally on the industrial life of our people that it is deemed proper to report the outstanding features of the situation. The amount of money in the fund held by the State as trustee for the injured workmen and their dependents, as of date, January 2, 1919, was $15,401,429.74. So carefully measured has been the cost of human justice that employers pay a smaller premium-rate in Ohio than elsewhere, and the injured workmen and their dependents are given larger compensation. A dramatic circumstance which bears eloquent testimony in behalf of this law is here recited: Not long since a workman was injured in a factory through which runs the boundary line between Ohio and Pennsylvania. The accident occurred a few feet east of our state, but the poor fellow crawled back onto the soil of Ohio because he knew the difference between our law and the law in Pennsylvania. As a further evidence of the basic soundness of the law and the character of its administration, I have directed the Industrial Commission to have an actuarial audit of the fund in its charge, with the imposed condition that the Ohio Federation of Labor, the Ohio Manufacturers' Association and the State Auditor be consulted in the employment of the most competent actuary, obtainable outside the state service, to do the work."

This, then, is the story, but not all of it. Having its genesis in the meetings between labor and capital, there has been worked out by the two an elaborate code of safety rules which have been officially promulgated by the commission and have the binding effect of law. To-day capital and labor will demand of his successor that his heart and mind be in accord with the program carried to fruition in his six years as Governor. There are other points in his service, briefly covered here, in these lists:

Laws Pertaining to Business

A public utilities law providing property re-valuation as a basis for rate making.

Provision for court appear from the utilities commission decision to the court of final jurisdiction, preventing delay and loss.

Prohibition against injunction on rate hearing without court investigation.

A uniform accounting system applied to utilities.

A state banking code with close co-operation with the federal reserve system, bringing all private banks under state supervision.

State expenditure on a budget system to reduce cost of government and lessen taxation.

A blue-sky act to encourage proper investment and protect against fraudulent securities.

Labor Legislation

A State Industrial Commission with powers to handle all questions affecting capital and labor, with a state mediator as the keystone.

Complete survey of occupational diseases with recommendation for health and occupational insurance.

Full switching crew in all railroad yards.

Strengthening the user in the state of railroad safety appliances.

A full crew law.

Twenty-four foot caboose.

Reduction of consecutive hours of employment for electric railroad workers.

Obstruction of fixed signals prohibited.

Safeguarding of accidents in mines by proper illumination.

Extra provision for dependents of men killed in mines.

Increased facilities for mine inspector operation.

Protection of miners working toward abandoned mines.

Elimination of sweatshop labor.

Provision for minimum time pay day.

Prohibition of contract labor in workhouses.

Provision for minimum wage and nine-hour working day for women.

Eight-hour working day on all public contracts.

Codification of child laws with establishment of child welfare department.

Compulsory provision for mothers' pensions.

Verdict by three-fourths jury in civil cases.

CHAPTER VII

THE LEADER OF THE STATE IN WAR—VISION IN GOVERNMENT IN PEACE TIME

Theodore Roosevelt said that Governor Cox was among the very foremost of war Governors. The utterance was made after he had assessed the things done during the fateful period of hostilities. Presenting complicated problems at all time it was no less true that in war there were major, not minor, obstacles to be met and surmounted before Ohio might take her traditional place as one of the very militant states of the Union. That she did achieve such place attests the zeal and ardor of the Governor. Ohio presented to the country a complete division, the Thirty-seventh, recruited under the personal supervision of Governor Cox. It led the nation, by long odds, in sale of war saving stamps, an activity stimulated by Governor Cox. It preserved good order and set an example in spite of many conflicting racial antagonisms within its borders by cultivation of such a spirit as made open or covert disloyalty dangerous to the disloyal. Withal there was no untoward incident affecting peaceful alien enemies. In the cities, none led those of Ohio in war gardening, and the tractor campaign for Ohio farms was adopted and imitated in other states. The Governor himself was a dynamo of activity, organizing the first State Council of Defense and enlisting volunteer aid at no expense to state and country in quickening all war and related activities. Every situation affecting the State's power found him ready for the emergency. When an early frost and severe winter in 1917-18 destroyed much of the seed corn, the Governor uncovered instances of profiteering and immediately stopped it by vigorous action. Corn in other districts with similar soil and climate was brought in and sold at three dollars a bushel.

Soldiers of no state were better supplied with all the comforts that could be provided than those of Ohio. While the Thirty- seventh was in camp in the far South a Christmas train was sent to it. Special funds were raised for entertainment of both the Ohio camps. In a word, every war activity felt the vigilant care and sympathetic help of the Governor.

During the war time there were few idle men in Ohio. Through proclamation attention of local authorities was directed to an old law making vagrancy an offense and it was applied rigorously.

No less in reconstruction than in was activities his energies were tireless. The Governor took the lead in securing legislation to correct the defects found in educational laws and one of the statutes placed upon the books at his suggestion provided for an oath of allegiance on the part of teachers. Referring to disclosures in certain cities, he said: "We have had our bitter experiences and love for our children compels us, in common prudence, to protect them."

Without sympathy for the mischievous spirits who sought to foment trouble in America, the Governor clearly expressed his conception of Americanization as a voluntary spiritual, and not a compulsory, process. The policy he had in mind was indicated in an address in Chicago in March, 1920, in which he said:

"There must be no compromise with treason, but the surest death to Bolshevism is exposure of the germ of the disease itself to the sunlight of public view. We must protect ourselves against extremes in America. The horrors and tragedies of revolution can be charged to them. If government is assailed, its policy must not become vengeful. Our fathers in specifying what human freedom was, and providing guarantees for its preservation, recognized that among the necessary precautions was the protection of individual right against governmental abuses.

"If the alien, ignorant of our laws and customs, cows in fear of our government, he is very apt to believe that things are much the same the world over, and he may become and easy convert to the doctrine of resistance. The skies will clear but meanwhile government must be firm, yet judicial, uninfluenced by the emotionalism that breeds extremes. The less government we have, consistent with safety to life and property, the better for both happiness and morals. A policeman on every corner would be a bad index to the citizenship of the community, for it would reflect a foolish concept of conditions by the municipal officers."

The vision of Governor Cox in legislation is best to be studied in the statute book of Ohio. The fact is that he was a pioneer in some of this, indeed in a large part of it. Through the years he has insisted that government must deal with its problem by evolution lest revolution overtake it. It was this sentiment that led him to deal with the industrial injury matter. When he heard men inveighing against the courts, a discerning eye knew something was wrong and he gave his attention to righting that wrong. His creed, not recently as a candidate, but in the years of his public career, has been expressed in this summary: "Our view is toward the sunrise of tomorrow with its progress and its eternal promise of better things."

The expression is found so frequently in his state documents that it might properly be set forth in the form of a creed. But there has been more than what the great Roosevelt called "lip- service to progress. The forward steps became a part of the laws.

In health affairs he asked for the appointment of a commission to study the need for adequate local administration and he urged its adoption before the General Assembly so forcefully that Ohio to-day has what is universally recognized to be the best system in America. In placing the state department upon a footing commensurate with other institutions of government, case was taken to place it where it cannot be prostituted to partisanship. There has been a growing number of governmental departments under Governor Cox in which partisanship is utterly forbidden. They include the Board of Administration, dealing with the wards of the state, the social agencies, the educational, and the Fish and Game Department. An actual census in all the varied public office activities in Ohio would disclose that although the Democratic party has been in possession of the Government for nearly all of the past twelve years, the number of members of the Republican party on the public rolls is almost as great as that of the victors. The Governor has found that men in the world of business employ, at larger compensation than the state has afforded, the type of men he has most often selected for responsible posts. It is one of the curious effects of progress in government that it has touched and awakened progress in business and in civic life.

In social service there has been evolved the cold storage act which has served as a model for proposed national legislation. under its provisions a strict limitation of time is placed upon the storing of food. With this has gone strict legislation against adulteration of food and honest enforcement of the laws.

Other states have accepted as a model the social agency committee now working in effective co-operation with state departments and bringing into mutual operation all recognized social agencies. One of the greatest steps forward was the establishment of a bureau of juvenile research with Dr. L. H. Goddard at its head.

Second to no other reform has been that effected in handling of the prison problem. Prisoners now earn their freedom through work in the healthful out-of-doors on highways, in plants for making road material, and on farms. There is a system of compensation to the families for work done as a balance on which to begin life anew.

Twelve hundred consolidated schools in Ohio attest the successful workings of the rural school code which was brought into existence in 1914 after careful study and after the state in general meetings had carefully studied the plans. The old one-room school house is giving way in the country to the modern centralized school and community life is being remade. Through the raising of the country school to the plane of those of the cities, it will be possible to check the alarming drift to the cities and depopulation of the countryside. Governor Cox does not believe that the federal government should interfere in the affairs of local communities but he does believe that it "can inventory the possibilities of progressive education, and in helpful manner create an enlarged public interest in this subject."

Along with the improvement of rural schools has gone a most comprehensive highway programme involving an annual outlay of millions of dollars. Gradually as highways are improved they will, under the state policy shaped in 1913, be taken over by the state.

The agricultural legislation was in consonance with the other subjects touched. Ohio was long a dumping ground for inferior fertilizers, diseased livestock and impure seed. Adequate laws have changed all this. Still, these are police measures not of necessity a true index of real vision in agricultural matters. The boldest step ever taken was the establishment of pure bred herds of cattle by the state with opportunity afforded through breeding service at institutional farms to extend these pure strains to the small farms. The success attained is reflected in numerous heard of thorough-bred cattle.

CHAPTER VIII

FIGHTING "SLUSH FUNDS"

Developments of the present campaign have given a peculiar interest to past history with respect to the record of Governor Cox in dealing with campaign expenditures. The Governor's reports, which have been filed under the Ohio Corrupt Practice law, show that he has never been an extravagant spender in campaigns. In his various races for the Governor's office in Ohio one of the points which he has claimed is the redemption of pledges made to the people. Under one of these pledges he advocated and secured the enactment of an anti-lobby law, designed to reduce the evils attendant upon the presence of a legislative lobby. He found upon the statute books of Ohio a corrupt practice act and this was strengthened by laws passed during his term. In taking hold as Governor in 1913, he demanded and secured a rigid lobby law. Of this he said:

"Conditions not only justify but demand drastic anti lobby law. Any person interesting himself in legislation will not, if his motive and cause be just, object to registering his name, residence and the matters he is espousing, with the secretary of state, or some other authority designated by your body. If his activities be of such nature that he does not care to reveal them in the manner indicated, then the public interest is obviously endangered. It is no more than a prudent safeguard to have it known what influences are at work with respect to legislation. There ought to be no temporizing with this situation."

In the first year of his administration he combated an attempt to annul the workmen's compensation law by an improper referendum and vigorously cleaned up the situation by causing the arrest of those who had conspired to falsify names to petitions. The Governor followed up his activity for clean administration of the referendum system by comprehensive laws in 1914, since when no abuses have been discovered. What he said to the General Assembly gave a further indication of his policy in this respect. He said:

"The underlying spirit of the corrupt practice laws in the state and nation is the ascertainment of the influences behind candidates or measures. We can with profit compel a sworn itemized statement when the petition is filed showing all money or things of value paid, given or promised for circulating such petitions."

In the campaign of 1916, in which Governor Cox was re-elected, assertions were made of large improper expenditure of money in defiance of the law. In the following January at the regular session of the General Assembly, the Governor indicated his position by calling for a special legislative inquiry. The statements he made furnish an interesting background for the developments of the year. At that time he said:

"Let me lay particular emphasis on the necessity of safeguarding the suffrage thought of the state from the dangers of corrupt influences. The sums of money expended for so-called political purposes are assuming such magnitude as to cause seemingly well- founded alarm, if not to justify the belief that the legitimate purpose of campaigning is being exceeded. Unfettered by law, this tendency might result in the waters of our free institutions being poisoned at their very base. Reduced to simple terms, the object of a campaign is to inform the voters on every subject that legitimately and germanely joins to the issues and the candidates. Any step beyond this, and any project opposed to it in motive, cannot but be regarded as dangerous. Human frailties should not be played upon by vast treasures of money advanced by men or movements whose huge disbursements can hardly be looked upon as of patriotic inspiration. It is not necessary to expend large amounts of money for the promotion of a worthy cause, and, inversely, any cause or candidacy having behind it unprecedented financial support is likely to be regarded with suspicion. It may, through legislation, be necessary to restrain irresponsible organizations whose existence and activities are born of a hidden design, conceived by some interest afraid to operate in the open. I recommend that a legislative committee of investigation be appointed with the power to employ counsel, and the authority to summon persons and papers and to swear witnesses in order that it might be known just what organizations have been entering into campaign activities, and how much money they expended and collected—also the names of the contributors. This should extend also to candidates. The facts as adduced will then be a safe guide as to the necessity of strengthening the corrupt practices act, or more rigorously enforcing existing law, or both."

The legislative session had hardly concluded before the war with Germany broke out and it was deemed unwise at that time to proceed to any agitation on the subject. The functions of the committee were, accordingly never fulfilled. Early in the year of 1920, the Governor gave warning of the report that huge funds were to be raised in this year for election purposes. At the very outset of his campaign in addressing the members of Democratic National Committee at Columbus, the Governor said:

"I hope I do violence to no member of this committee when I submit to you this proposal: That we purpose not only to deal with eminent good faith with the electorate of this nation in November with reference to platform pledges, but we mean to let every man and woman understand where every dollar comes from, and for what purpose it is spent. We not only urge that as a matter of high principle, but in order to guarantee the triumph of our cause which deserves to triumph. We do not want the publication of expenditures after the election. There is no point in advising the voters what has been done. We want them to be fully advised of every circumstance with reference to the collection and the disbursement of funds in order that from the circumstances they can gain a correct index, and understand that when the Democracy is continued in power in Washington, it assumes its responsibility without a single obligation except to the conscience that God has given us.

"Therefore, gentlemen, let us make up a budget which will carry the full details and information—recounting the legitimate expenses of this campaign, render an accounting daily or weekly, and the source from which it came. And more than that, we shall insist upon the senatorial investigating committee continuing in session until the ballot has been closed in November. You know full well that a campaign fund sufficient in size to stagger the sensibilities of the nation is now being procured by our opponents. If they believe that is correct in principle, God speed them in the enterprise, It will be one of our chief assets in this campaign."

This, then is the record.

CHAPTER IX

THE LIFE STORY

Born at Jacksonburg, Ohio, March 31, 1870, son of Gilbert and Eliza Cox; educated in public schools; reared on farm; worked in printer's office; taught country school; became newspaper reporter; secretary to Congressman Sorg, 3d Ohio District; bought Dayton Daily News, 1898, and Springfield Press Republic, 1903, forming News League of Ohio; member 61st and 62d Congress (1909-13), 3d Ohio District; Governor of Ohio; elected in 1912, defeated in 1914, elected in 1916 and 1918; now serving third term; home, Trailsend, Dayton.

The family of Cox seems to have had its origin in England in the generations gone, but its Americanism is of two centuries in duration. At Freeboard, New Jersey, lived General James Cox, one of the early speakers of the New Jersey House of Representatives and later a member of Congress. Tillers of the soil and artisans, the closer forbears attained to no distinction in public life. To Ohio the family came sometime in the early years of the last century, and at Jacksonburg the paternal grandfather, Gilbert Cox, established himself. On the ancestral farm of 160 acres, his son, Gilbert, Jr., lived, and on it James M. Cox first saw the light of day. His uncles and aunts, for his father was one of a family of thirteen, were of the people who migrated westward. The youngest of a family of seven children, he learned the routine of tasks of a boy on the farm. In the little one-room country school he attended, his teachers found him an ordinary pupil but with a fondness for newspaper reading.

Cox's first public job was the humble position of janitor in the United Brethren Church, and even now his favorite reminiscence is the difficulty he had in making the old wood stove function properly. The thrifty farmers in those days were accustomed to commute part of their dues in cord wood for the church, and often the quality they supplied was not of the best. The boy became a member of the Church, a membership which is still retained.

At fifteen he left the elementary school to enter the Middletown High School, living with his sister, Mrs. John Q. Baker, whose husband was a teacher in the High School and owner of the Middletown Signal. Board was paid in working as a printer's devil until the apprenticeship was served and the county newspaper business was mastered from both the counting room and the editorial side. Upon completion of his high school course, the young man passed the county examination and obtained a position as teacher of the school he had in earlier years attended, but a pedagogical career was not to his liking and he returned to work on the Signal staff. He became also the local correspondent for the Cincinnati Enquirer and attracted the attention of the main office by a neat scoop which he landed regarding a railroad wreck. Graduating into the reportorial work, he became assistant telegraph and railroad editor of the Enquirer. He retired from the newspaper life for a time to become Secretary to Congressman Sorg, remaining in his capacity until his 28th year, when he purchased the Dayton News, giving $12,000 in notes and beginning with a capital of just $80. The times were hard enough for the young chap with creditors constantly upon him. Once his paper was forced to suspend by reason of an unpaid bill, and the opposition paper heralded its death. The struggling publisher retaliated with an "extra" announcing its continuance. Then again there were plenty of libel suits for the young editor-publisher, setting out to be a reformer, and the ruling powers in the city strongly disapproved his methods, but the militant editor brought readers and the readers brought advertisers, and the venture became a success. Five years from his first venture he bought the Springfield Press Republic and the Springfield Democrat, combining the two in the Evening News. Each is now housed in its own modern newspaper building and each is highly prosperous as a business institution, although the owner's supervision has been of a general character.

His associates always speak of the "Cox luck" in politics, but upon analysis it seems that it consists either of seizing or making the opportunity. In 1908 his Congressional district, originally Democratic, had become Republican, but a factional quarrel breaking out in the opposition camps, the Governor took the Democratic nomination and won out, again riding to victory in the great landslide of 1910. In Congress his career afforded him no opportunity to attain to high distinction, but he became a member of the appropriations committee and there became most deeply impressed with the waste in public funds and the unbusinesslike methods of arriving at appropriations. One of his services was the disclosure that the care of Civil War veterans in the National Soldiers' Home at Dayton was shattered, and he won the contest for increased allowances. The gratitude of the veterans was expressed in a majority from the Home in his re- election in 1910, thus breaking an historical precedent.

Two years later he became the champion of the constitutional amendments proposed by the Fourth Constitutional Convention of Ohio, then sitting, and as such was unanimously nominated by his party for Governor, on a platform which demanded a "new order" of things in Ohio. As soon as he was nominated he took the platform before the people for the adoption of the constitutional amendments in a special September election. These amendments included one providing for the initiative and referendum of which he had been an advocate for years, and one for the removal of officials failing to enforce the laws, giving the Governor the weapon with which he established his law- enforcement record. There was very little to the campaign in that year, the historical Republican party splitting in two upon the issue of progressiveness, and he was elected by an enormous plurality. Facing the tasks imposed by the new constitution, the Governor insisted upon legislative fulfillment of each popular mandate, and in a busy session of three months he accomplished his programme.

Aside from the legislation suggested by the amendments, his greatest constructive step was the enactment of a budget system, which sought to place the financial affairs of Ohio upon a businesslike basis. Its worth as a saver of money and promoter of efficiency has never been challenged. The previous Ohio fiscal system had grown grossly archaic. Appropriations were made by the Legislature to the departments in lump sums or in the form of granting all receipts and balances, some of the departments being maintained by the fees from interests they regulated. Of the departments having receipts of their own, many had deposits of their own in banks and their own checking accounts, so that their funds never passed through the State Treasury or through the hands of the State Auditor. Other departments got much or little from the Legislature, depending upon whether they had a gifted representative to appear for them before the legislative finance committee. Institutions vied with each other in providing the best entertainment to these committees as they made their week-end junket trips over the State during legislative sessions.

All this was changed in one sweeping stroke in the first administration of Governor Cox. All receipts of all departments now go into the State Treasury and none leave the treasury until it is appropriated in specific sums for specific purposes within specific departments. The state auditor has a check on every expenditure.

The Ohio budget department is composed of one commissioner appointed by the Governor, an assistant and a clerk. All departmental requests for funds desired of the next succeeding Legislature are filed with the Budget Commissioner, to be brought before the Governor. He investigates all items, ascertains the reasons for any increases that are asked, and fixes the sums he deems proper. Also, he estimates what the State revenues during the next biennium will be and prunes the budget to come within the total of expected revenues. The budget as prepared by the commissioner is submitted to the Governor, who frequently makes changes of his own after advising with department heads.

The Governor then presents the budget to the Legislature, which refers it to the finance committees of the two houses. The committees, and, in turn, the Legislature, have full authority to make any alterations, increases or decreases, desired, but the spellbinding by department representatives and wire-pulling by lobbyists are reduced to a minimum because the Budget Commissioner sits as the agent of the Governor at all sessions of the finance committees and at all times is prepared to defend the allowance he thinks a department should have.

The first budgetary appropriation bill repealed an existing appropriation law. It reduced appropriations aggregating $9,709,288 to $8,762,664, a saving of $946,624. Since that time the Ohio budget system has effected savings of millions, not, of course, in the sense that expenditures of the State government now are less than in 1913—for they have increased as governmental activities have enlarged—but in the sense that expenditures each year have been vastly less than they would have been without the budget plan of pruning and scaling down demands of existing State departments with a view both to general economy and avoidance of deficits.

The Ohio Budget and consequently its appropriation law classifies expenditures in two divisions: (1) Operating expenses and (2) Capital outlay (or permanent improvements).

Operating expenses are subdivided into personal service and maintenance. Personal service in turn is divided into salaries and wages, and maintenance into supplies, materials, equipment, contract or open order service, and fixed charges and contributions.

Elasticity of funds within departments is afforded by periodical meetings of a board of control, composed of the Governor (who may be and usually is represented by the Budget commissioner), the State Auditor, the Attorney-General, and the chairmen of the two legislative finance committees. If any new need develops within departments, funds for the purpose may be provided by a four-fifths vote of the board of control. Effort first is made to transfer the needed funds from one classification to another within the department. If no fund within the department has a surplus, and the need is great enough, relief may be granted by the emergency board, having the same membership as the board of control, which has at its disposal an emergency fund for contingencies arising between legislative sessions. Perfection never has been claimed for the Ohio system. Governor Cox himself realizes certain weaknesses in it and is making a fight now for strengthening features, which, however, necessitate a change in the constitution. One defect is that, regardless of probable income, the Legislature may increase items in the budget (or rather the appropriation bill based on the budget), and it may make other appropriations in separate bills as it sees fit without regard to prospective revenues.

In his 1919 message to the General Assembly, a Republican body, the Governor urged submission to the people of an amendment to the constitution providing that the Legislature shall have the right to diminish any item in the executive budget by majority vote or to strike out any item: that, however, it shall not be privileged to increase any item or to add a new one unless it makes legislative provision for sufficient revenue to meet the added cost. Such an amendment was not submitted. Unless it is done by an early legislature, adherents of Cox in Ohio say it may be undertaken by initiative petition.

Good Roads

Another notable achievement of Governor Cox is the advance of the Ohio highway system. Roads were in deplorable shape when he became Governor. There was no hope for rural counties with small tax duplicates, the ones in greatest need of good roads never being able to lift themselves out of the mud except through liberal state aid.

One of the Governor's first acts was a survey of road conditions. A complete network of 10,000 miles of inter-county roads was mapped out. It connected the eighty-eight county seats. Of the 10,000 miles of inter-county highways, 3000 miles, connecting the larger cities, were designated as main market roads. The scheme of financing called for improvement of the main market roads entirely at state expense, which the remainder of the system was to be built on a fifty-fifty basis, the state furnishing half the funds, and the county in which the road lies, the other half.

All road improvement under the Cox administration has been given such an impetus that the State, county and township programmes to-day call for an expenditure of $30,000,000 annually, including federal aid. Popular demand for highway improvement is greater than the State Highway department and county commissioners are able to meet.

Revitalizing the Schools

As a pupil in a one-room country school and as a teacher, he had first knowledge of the shortcomings and possibilities of the Ohio educational system. It was his firm conviction that the country boy and girl should be given the same educational advantages that accrued to those of the city.

The purpose of the Governor's school programme was to give Ohio a co-ordinates system of State, county and district supervision, to require normal or college training of all teachers, and, above all, to pave the way for speedier centralization and consolidation of the one-room district school. Results have been beyond the expectations of school men, every breath and opposition to the system has blown away, and it may truthfully be said that it has become an idol of the people of the state. The re-organization has stimulated interest in education in all respects and has made possible a more recent establishment of a state-wide teachers' pensions system and a complete revamping of financial support of schools through a State and county aid plan. Salaries of teachers have been increased the last six years from a minimum of $40 a month to a statutory minimum of $800 a school year. The teacher shortage occasioned by the war will be solved without much delay in Ohio, as county and state normal schools report prospective increases in attendance of fifty to one hundred per cent or even greater for next year.

The time had come in 1913 when the little district school with its narrow curriculum and crude methods of instruction did not meet the needs and purposes of modern industrial and social life in Ohio. It had not kept step with rural economic progress. In the whole State it was the one evidence of retardation, an institution of bygone days which had deteriorated instead of having improved. The right of every child to educational opportunities for development to the fullest extent of his possibilities was not recognized by the State in the school system as it existed at that time. Governor Cox, in his first message to the general assembly in January, 1913, recommended that a complete school survey be made. A survey commission was created To acquaint school patrons with the object of the survey in progress and to get them to discuss in their own communities the defects and the needs of the schools, November 14, 1913, was set apart as "School survey day" and a light burned in every school building in the State that night. Delegates were appointed to attend a state-wide educational congress the next month, and in January, 1914, the Governor called a special session to enact the rural school code.

The survey report disclosed that not half of the teachers of the State ever had attended high school, nor had normal training. Rural schools were mere stepping stones for young teachers before securing positions in village and city schools, agriculture was scarcely taught, schools were without equipment, three-fourths of the buildings were twenty years old or older, unsanitary, poorly lighted, without ventilation and insufficiently heated.

With one stroke the new school code created county supervision districts under the control of county boards, elected by the presidents of village and township boards; provided for county superintendents and supervisors over smaller districts within the county; required academic and professional training of all new teachers henceforth, and gave communities wider powers to centralize and consolidate schools.

At present ninety-five per cent of the elementary teachers have had professional training, and high school teachers are required to be college graduates or have equivalent scholastic attainment. The most common faults of class-room instruction have been to a great extent eliminated. Standard methods of presentation are being practices in an attempt to give to each child opportunity for development of his possibilities.

A great stimulation of public school sentiment is manifested by a closer co-operation and correlation of the school and the home, resulting in boys' and girls' club work, achievement courses, home projects and other school extension and community activities; a growth of the feeling of responsibility to the community on the part of the teacher; an attitude of greater interest and responsibility of the boards of education toward the school; a willingness of the people to vote money for new school plants and enterprises; a growing demand for consolidation and centralization; a better trained class of teachers, increased school attendance, especially in high schools where it has increased from fifty to one hundred per cent.

School administration is much more efficient as is demonstrated by a uniform course of study for elementary and high schools, vitalized by its articulation with the industrial activities of the community, county uniformity of textbooks, selection and correlation of textbook material and its adaptation to the varying interests and needs of childhood, uniform system of reports and records, and the like.

School centers have been made to coincide with social and business centers. Convenient districts have been formed around centers of population. village and surrounding rural districts have been united in accordance with the trend of the community interests and activities. Weak districts have been eliminated by the transfer of their territory to other districts, thereby strengthening property valuations.

A centralized school in Ohio was almost a novelty in 1914. A year ago there were 310 centralized (township) schools and 599 consolidated (embracing several contiguous districts) schools, and the number has been materially swelled during the year. Seventy of the eighty-eight counties now have such schools and the trend is toward them throughout the State. One such school replaces, on the average, eight one-room schools. They have brought to the rural pupils trained teachers, well-equipped buildings, courses of study related to the interests of the farm and home by being well-balanced between the cultural and vocational. They have made it possible for the country boy who remains on the farm to obtain a high school education in his own community that is directly related to his needs. Scientific agriculture under trained instructors is taught in all of these schools. The possibilities of the farm and of rural life are thus revealed to the boy and he will be equipped with knowledge necessary to the scientific performance of his work. From the farm instead of the law office and the counting room will come those who know what the needs and interests of the farmer are and who will be qualified to represent those interests.

While the system still may be said to be in its infancy, the progress of transformation of Ohio schools under it has been nothing short of wonderful, and unending results may be expected of it.

This extensive legislation had aroused many prejudices particularly, in the rural sections, of which his opponent, Congressman Frank B. Willis, took advantage. The bold challenge of the Governor to his opponent was stated by him on the platform in many parts of Ohio "Which law will you repeal?" The question was never answered, but the tide of opposition to the changes swept Governor Cox out of office, although he ran many thousands ahead of his associates. In the succeeding sessions of the General Assembly popular sentiment began once more to swing to Governor Cox and two years later he was re-elected by a small plurality. Improvement in the various laws was sought during his next term, but the shadow of the world war was already beginning to fall, and the greater part of his efforts were devoted to preparation for Ohio's part.

In general administration the Governor's supporters are fond of saying that he met successfully

> In his first term a flood,
> In his second term a war,
> In his third term reconstruction.

The flood story was the one that really introduced him first to the country at large. Ohio was hit by a calamity greater than any that had befallen a state. Columbus, Dayton, Marietta, Hamilton and other cities were under water for days, many villages were almost washed off the map, and hundreds of lives and untold millions of property were lost. Bridges everywhere were washed out and transportation was practically at a standstill. The eyes of the State and Country were on the then untried Governor Cox. He met the situation in a manner that will never be forgotten in Ohio. The Ohio National Guard was called out, stricken communities were placed under martial law, civilian relief armies under the command of mayors and other designated leaders organized everywhere, Ohio's motor truck, automobile and other facilities commandeered, and the work of feeding, clothing, cleaning up and rehabilitation carried on from the beginning with astounding efficiency.

The New York World at that time said of him:

"The man who has dominated the situation in Ohio is Governor Cox. He has been not only chief magistrate and commander-in-chief, but the head of the life-saving service, the greatest provider of food and clothing the

State has ever known, the principal health officer, the sanest counselor, the severest disciplinarian, the kindest philanthropist and best reporter. He has performed incredible labors in all these fields, and his illuminating dispatches to the World at the close of the heart- breaking days have given a clearer vision of conditions than could be had from any other source. Reared on a farm, educated in the public schools, a printer by trade, a successful publisher and editor of newspapers, a great Governor and a reported who gets his story into the first edition, James M. Cox excites and is herewith offered assurance of the World's most distinguished consideration."

The flood revealed the necessity for conservancy legislation and the measure recommended by the Governor was enacted to give local communities the right to protect themselves.

The time has gone by when in Ohio the major things in the programme of Governor Cox can be attacked successfully before the people of the State. He does not claim perfection. Suggestion as to improvement has found him ready to listen. There is still a short time for him to serve, but the public judgment has been made up, and Buckeye citizens, without regard to party affiliation, says that he has been a "good Governor."